I0431476

TATTO

coloring book

for adult

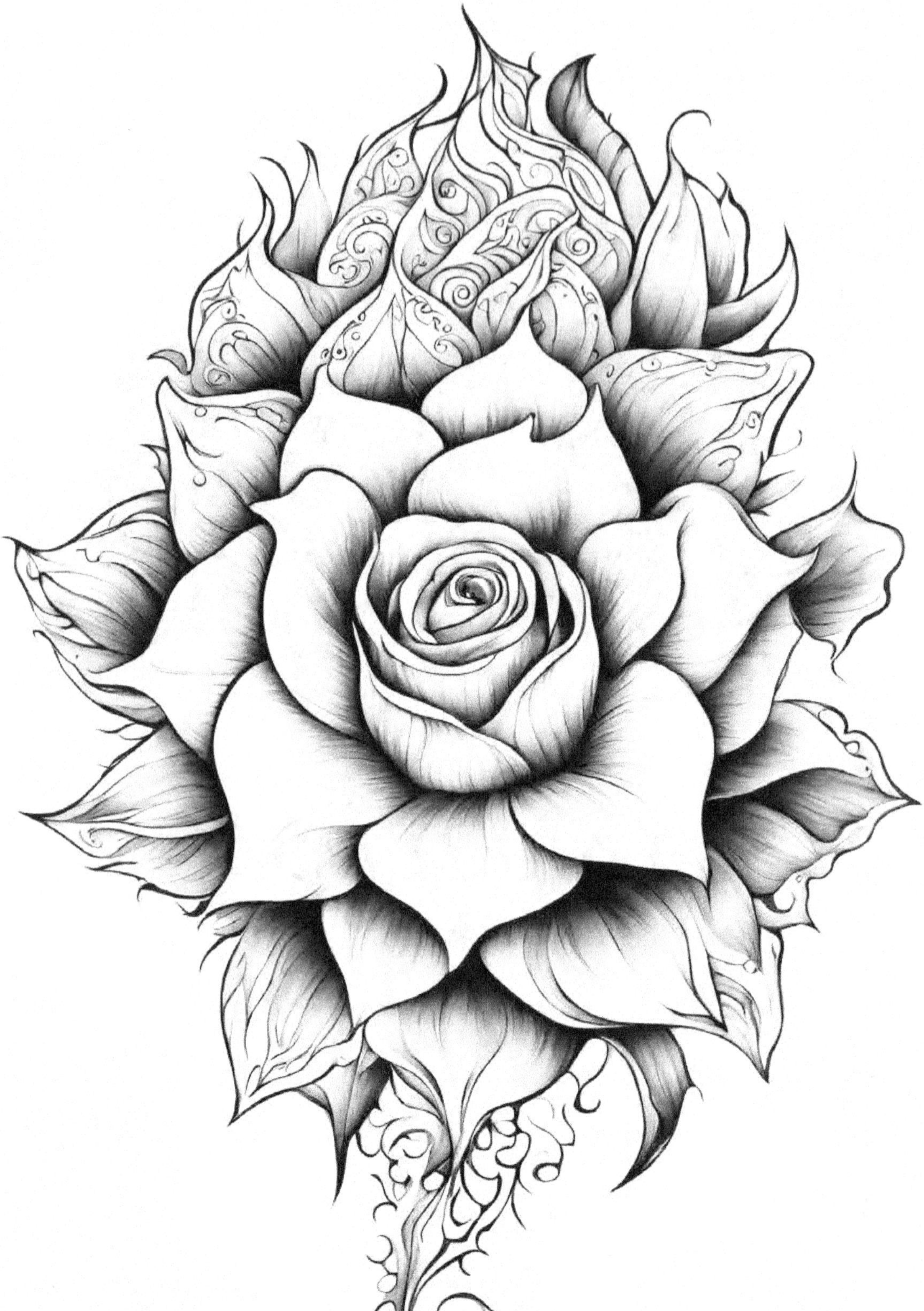

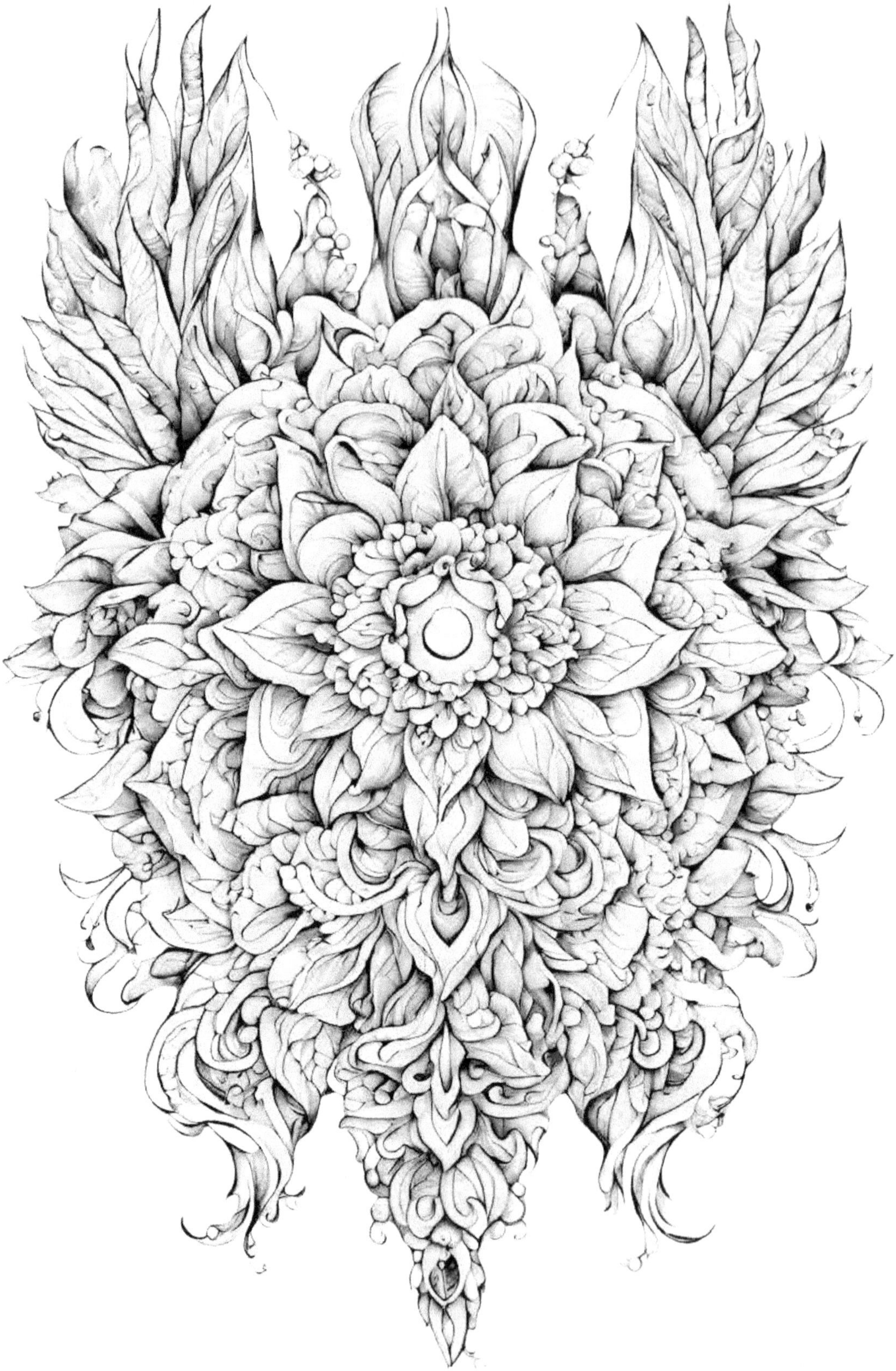

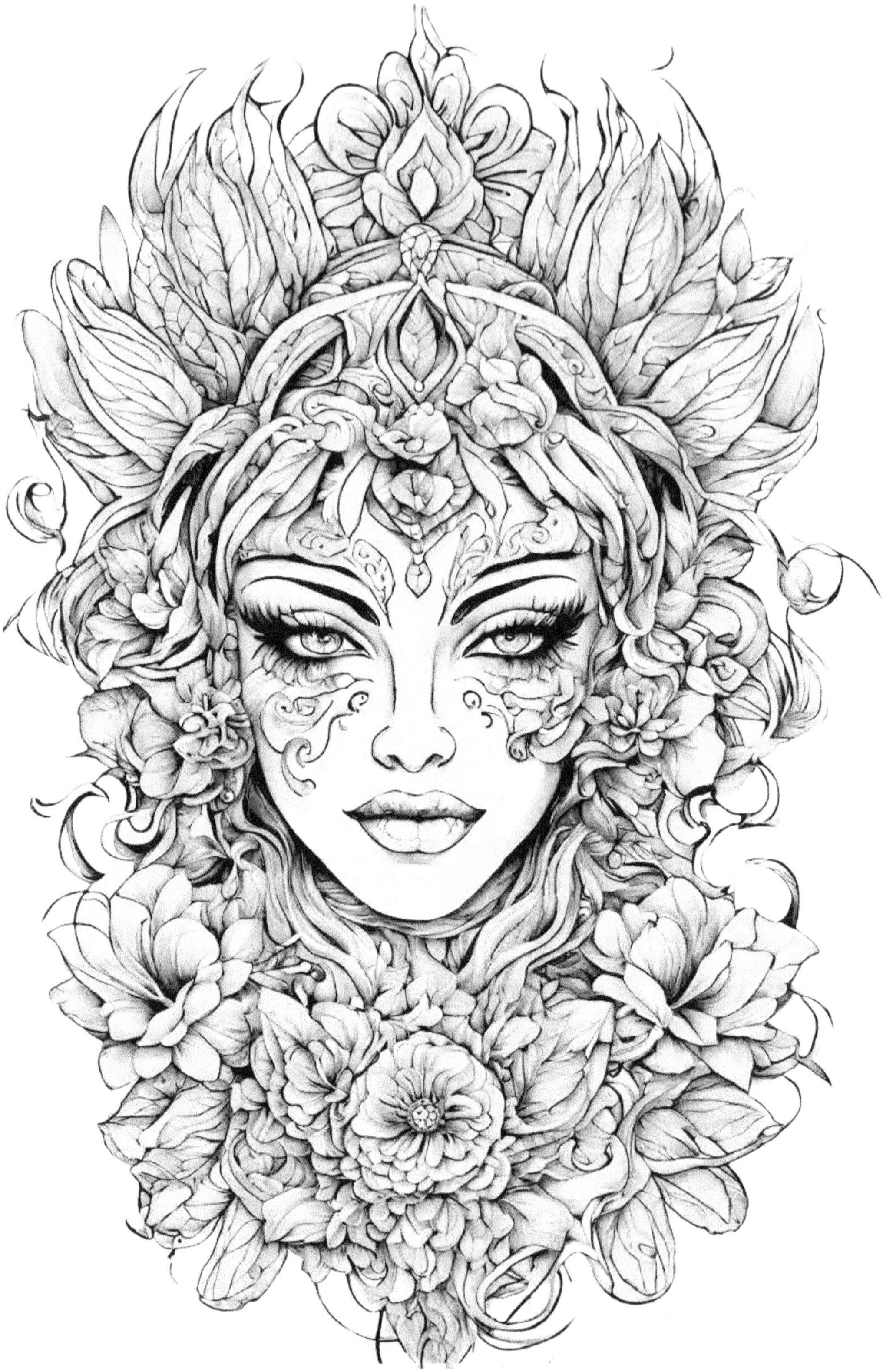

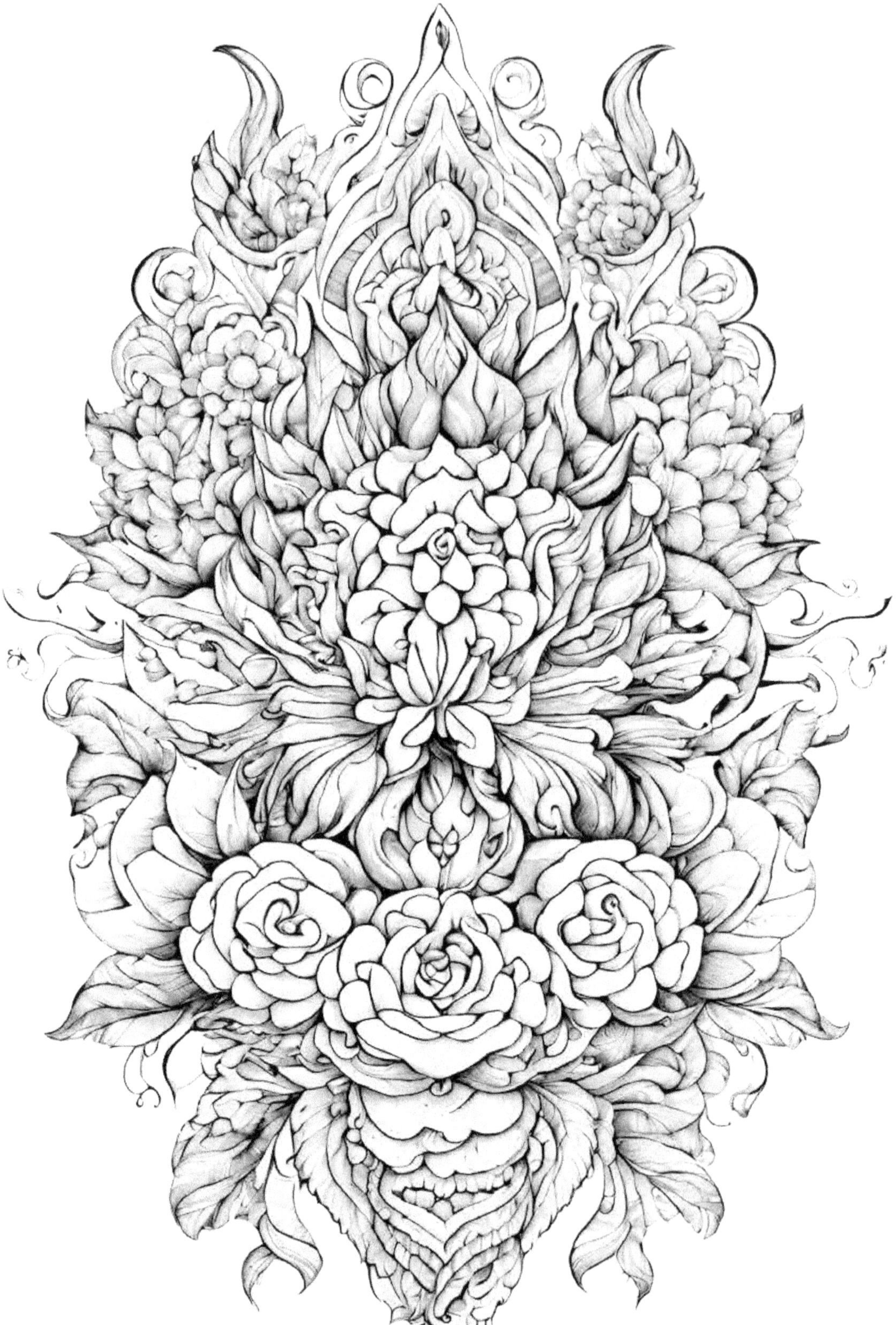

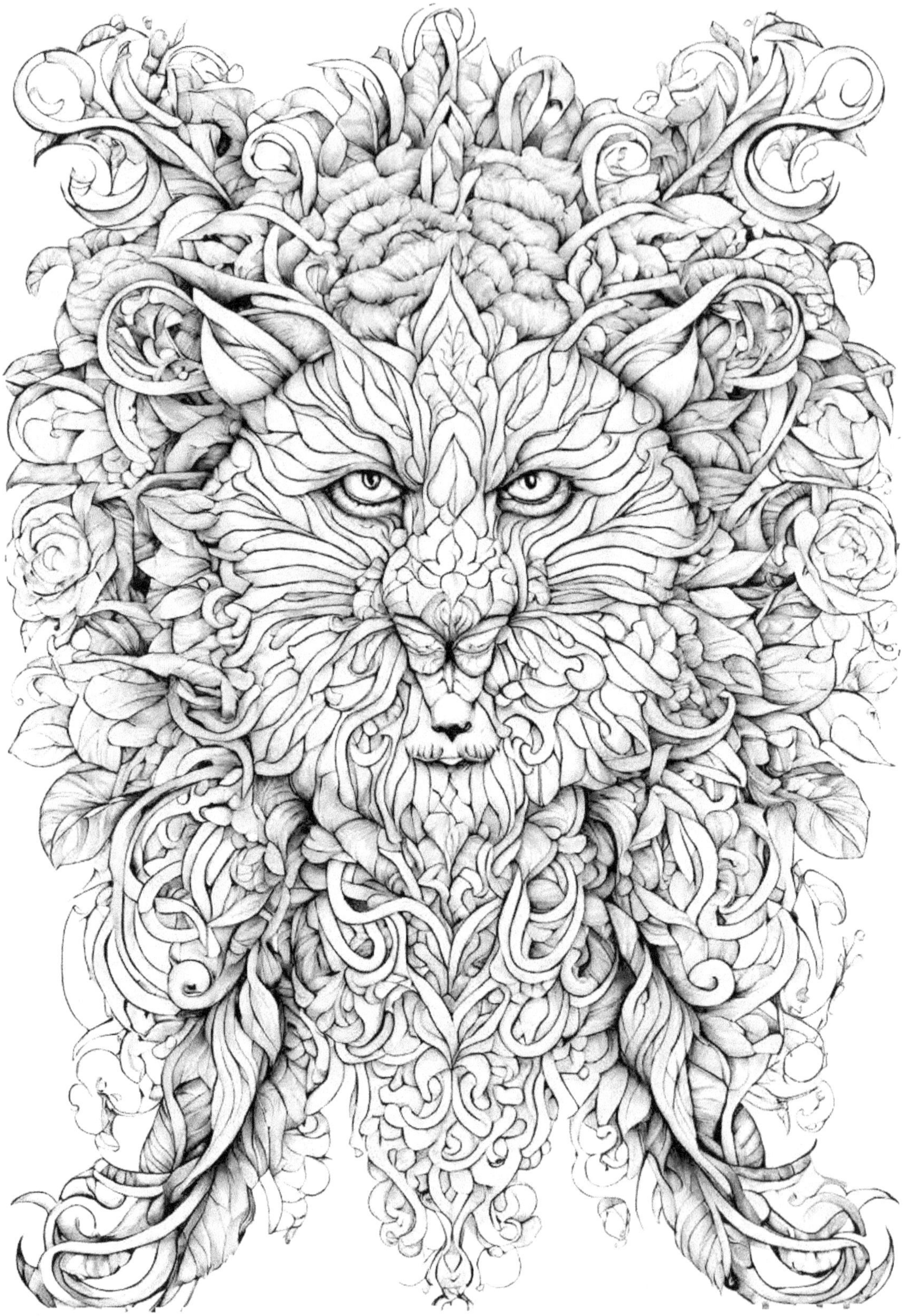

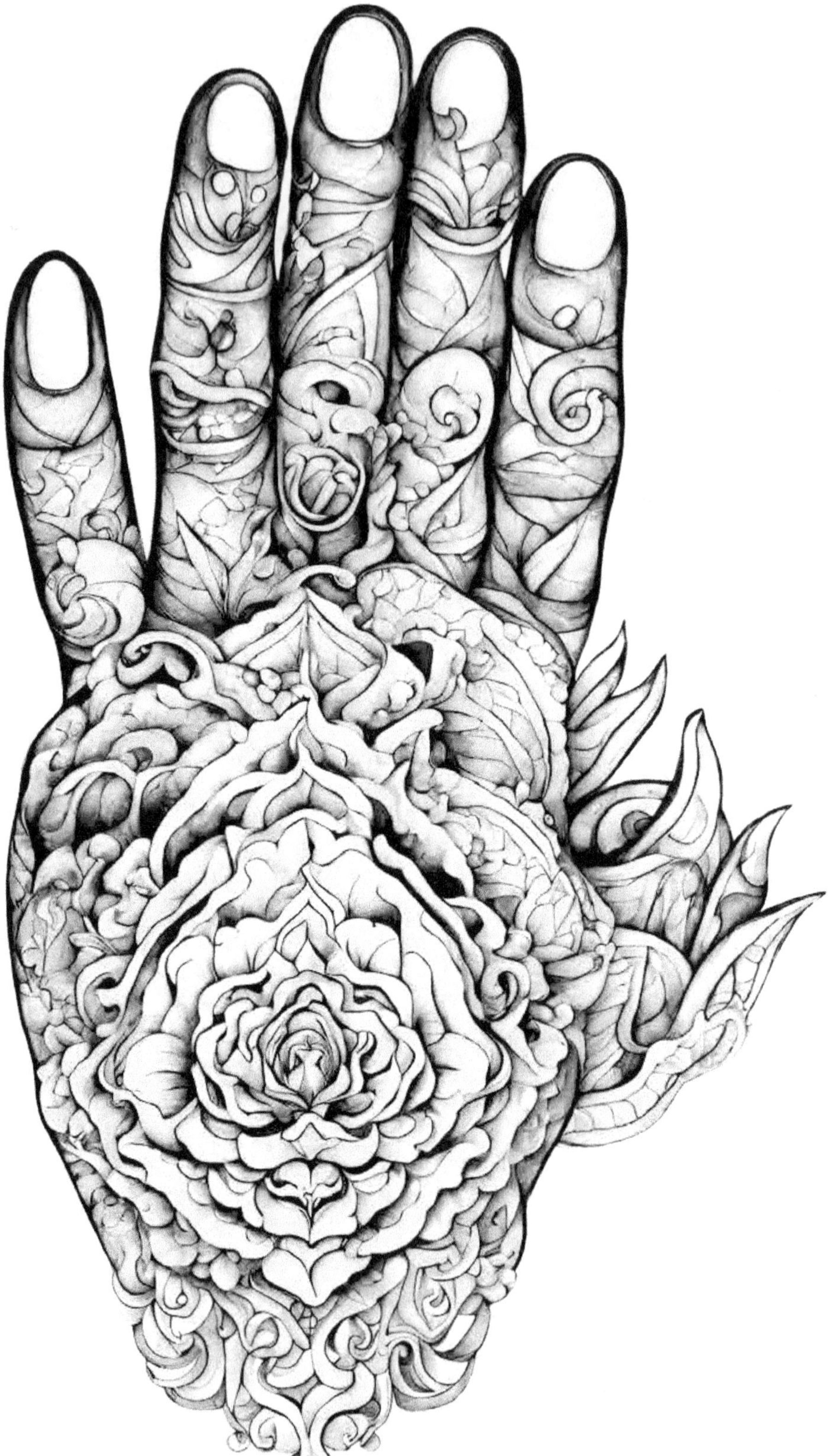

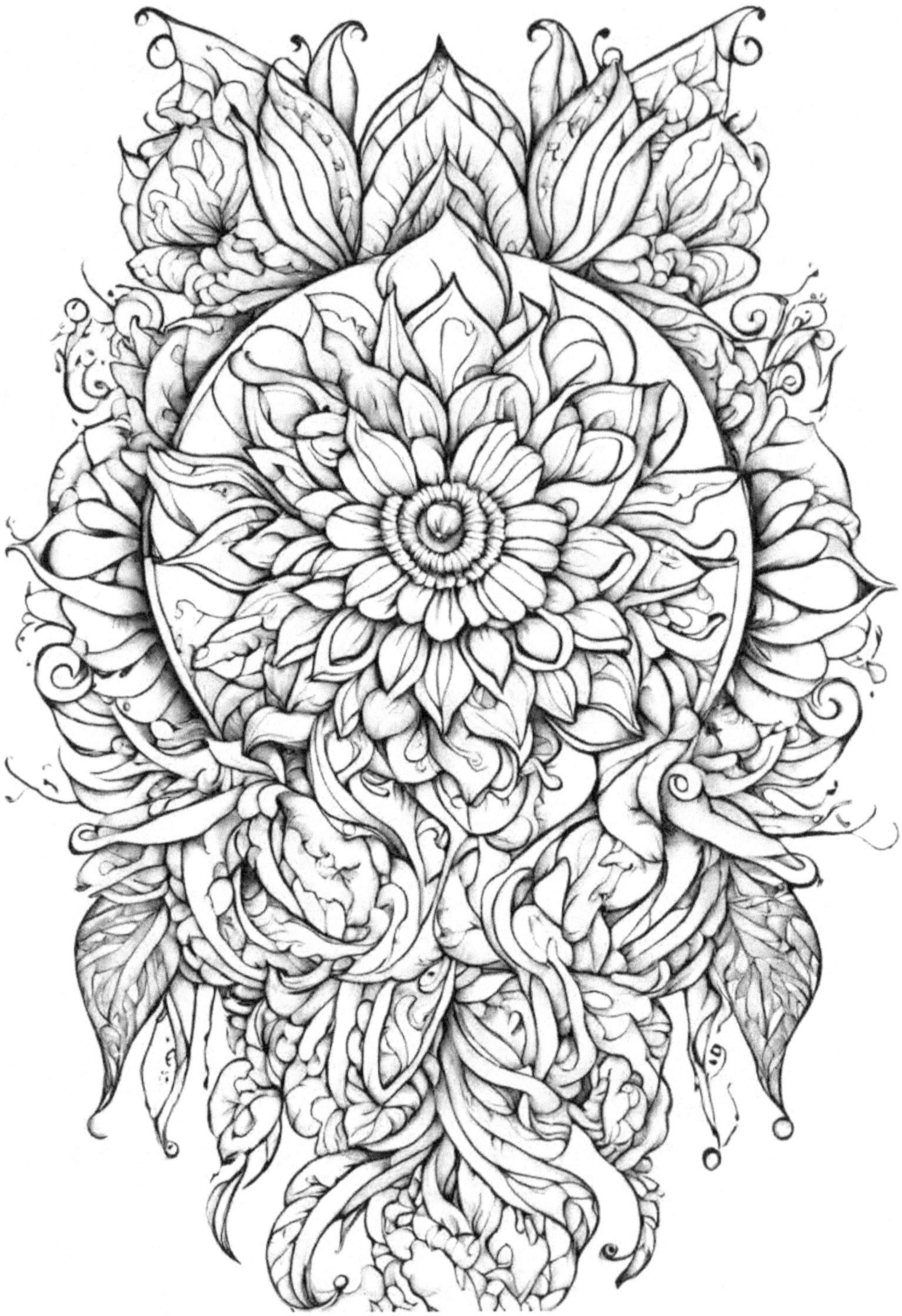

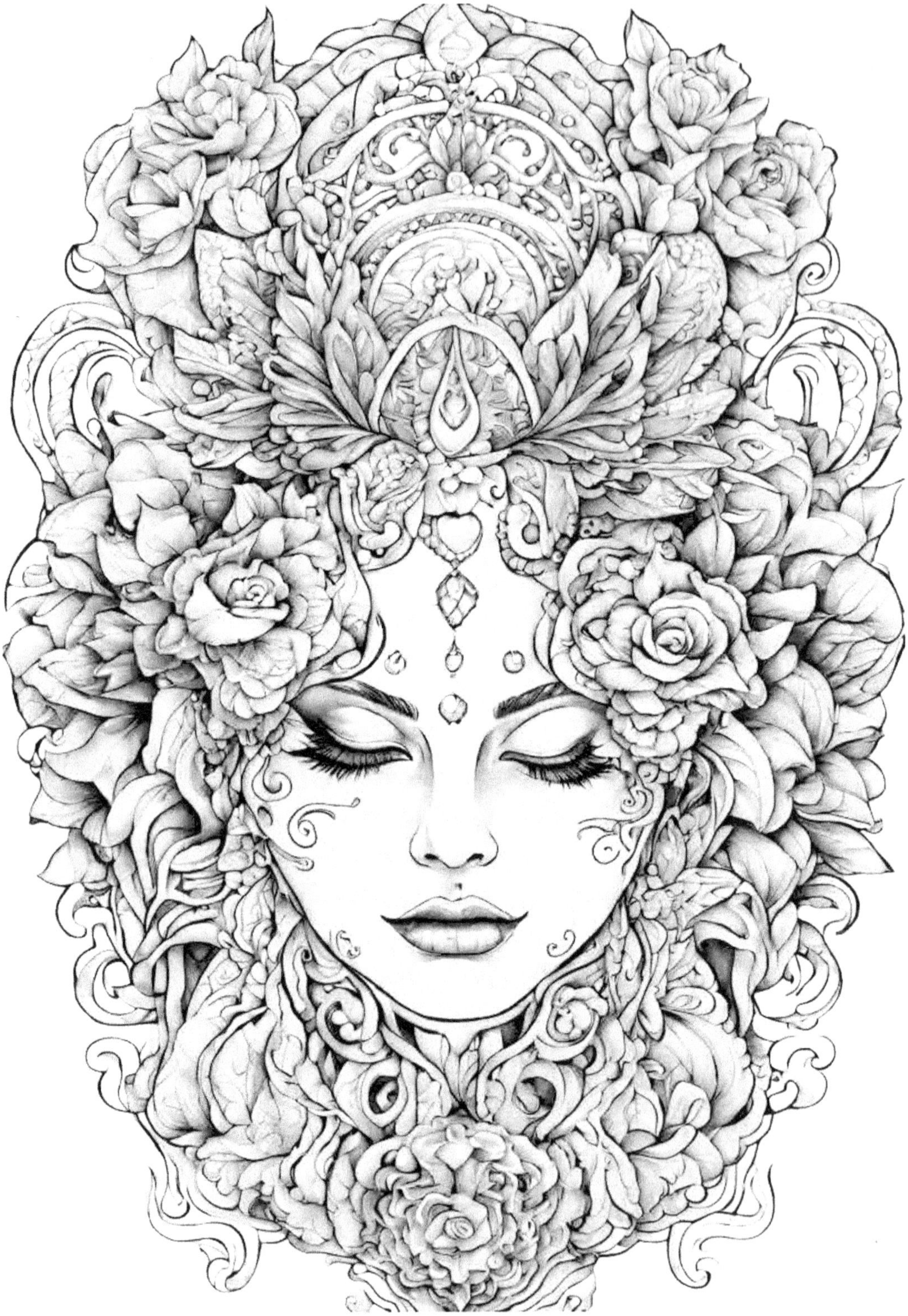

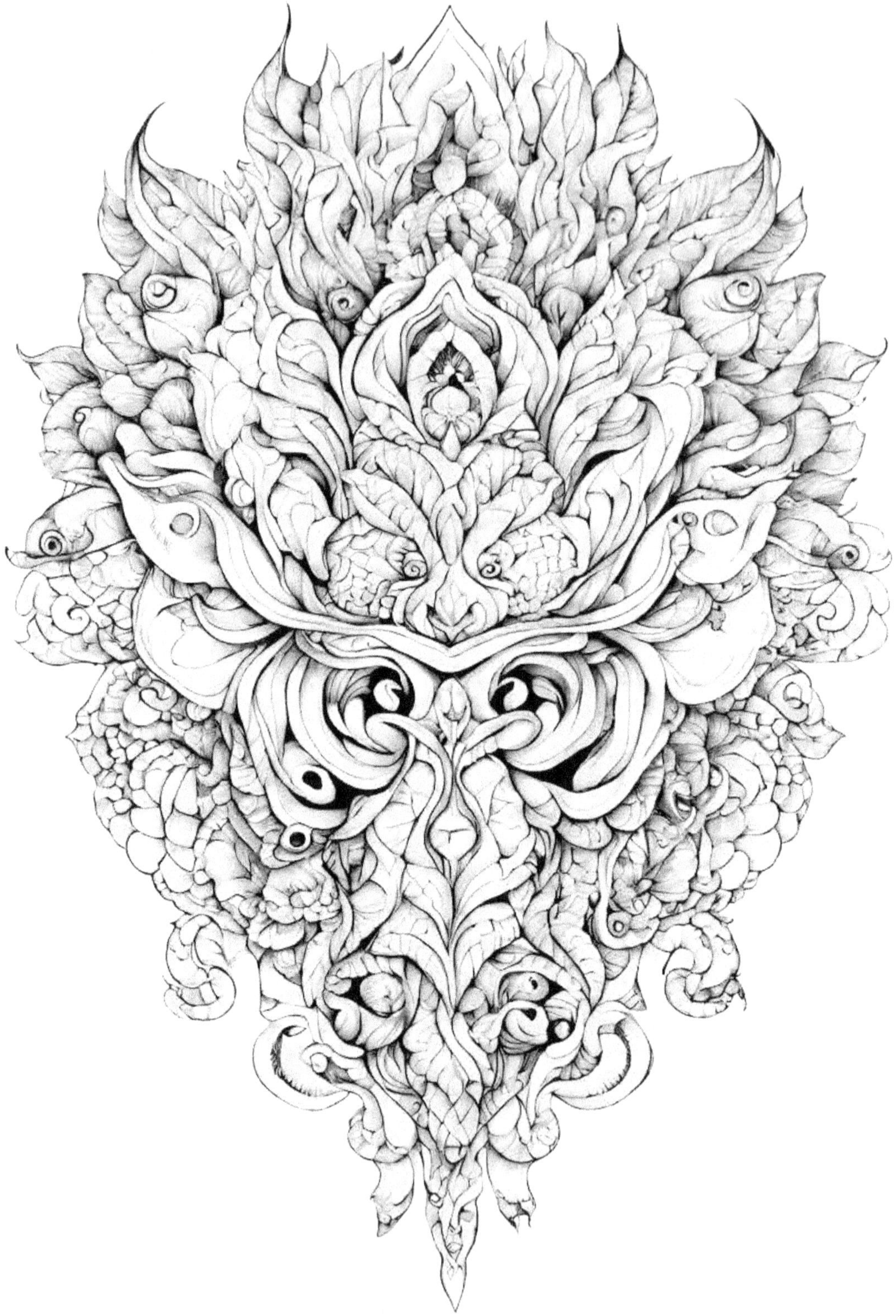

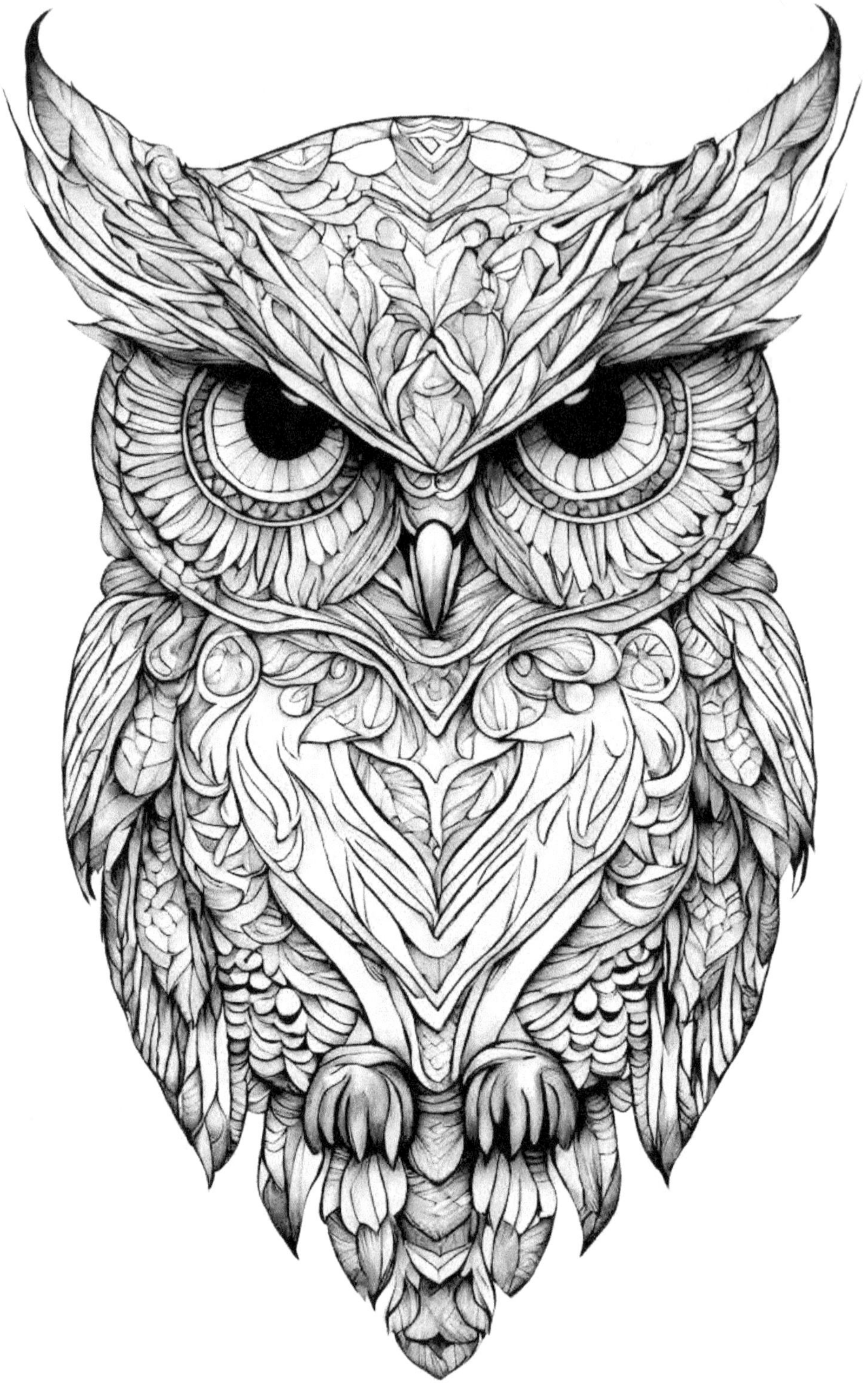

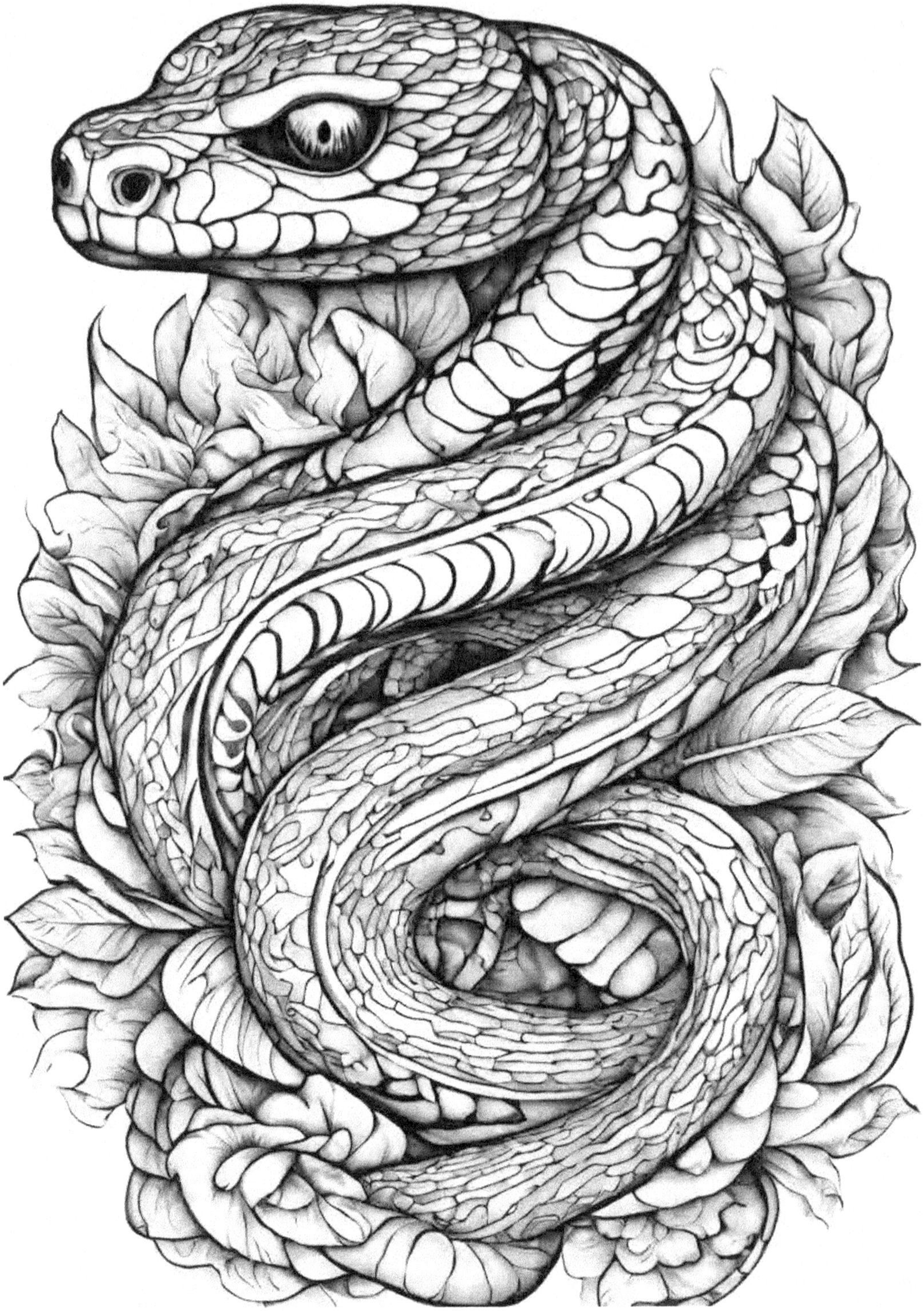

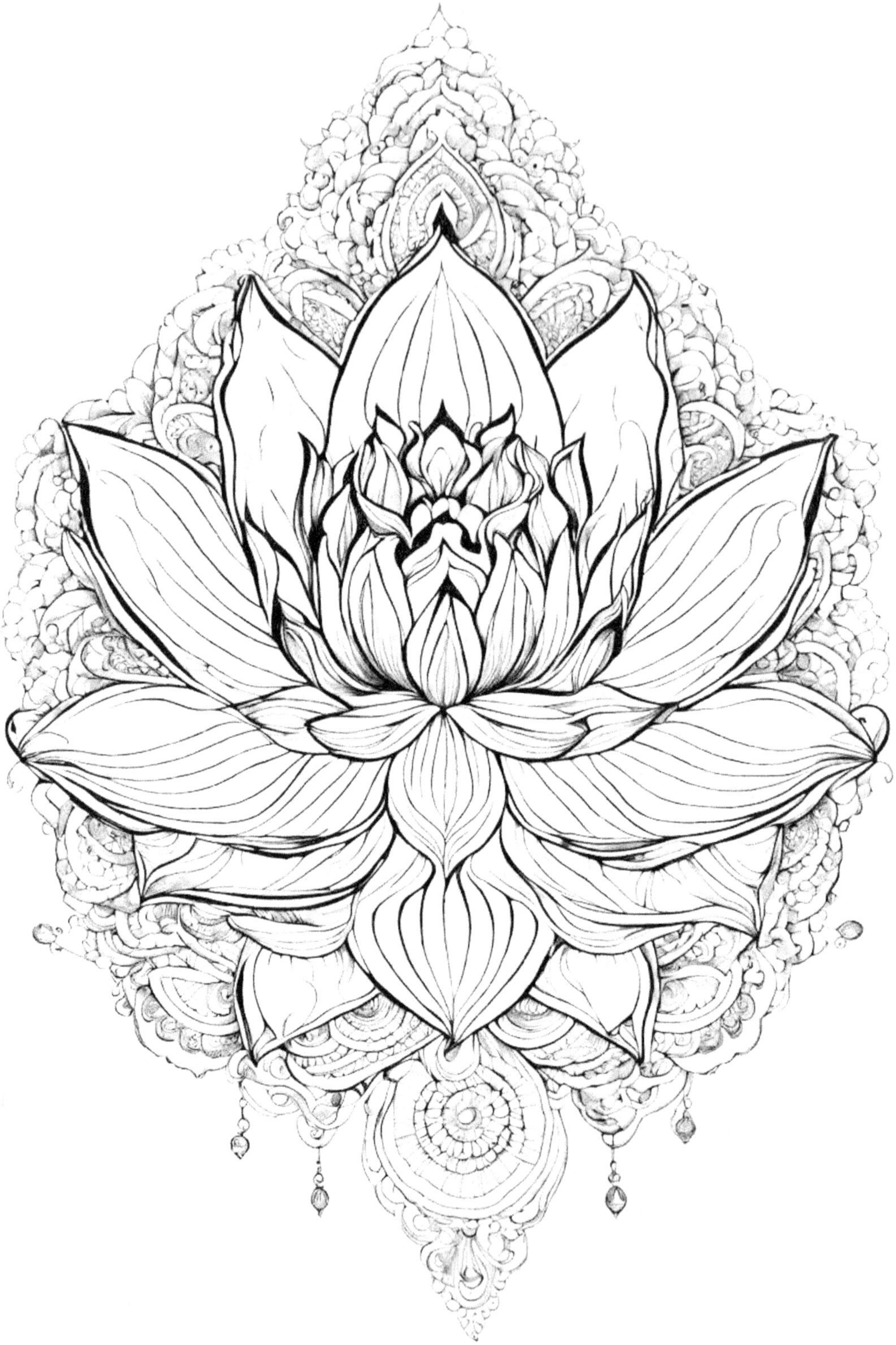

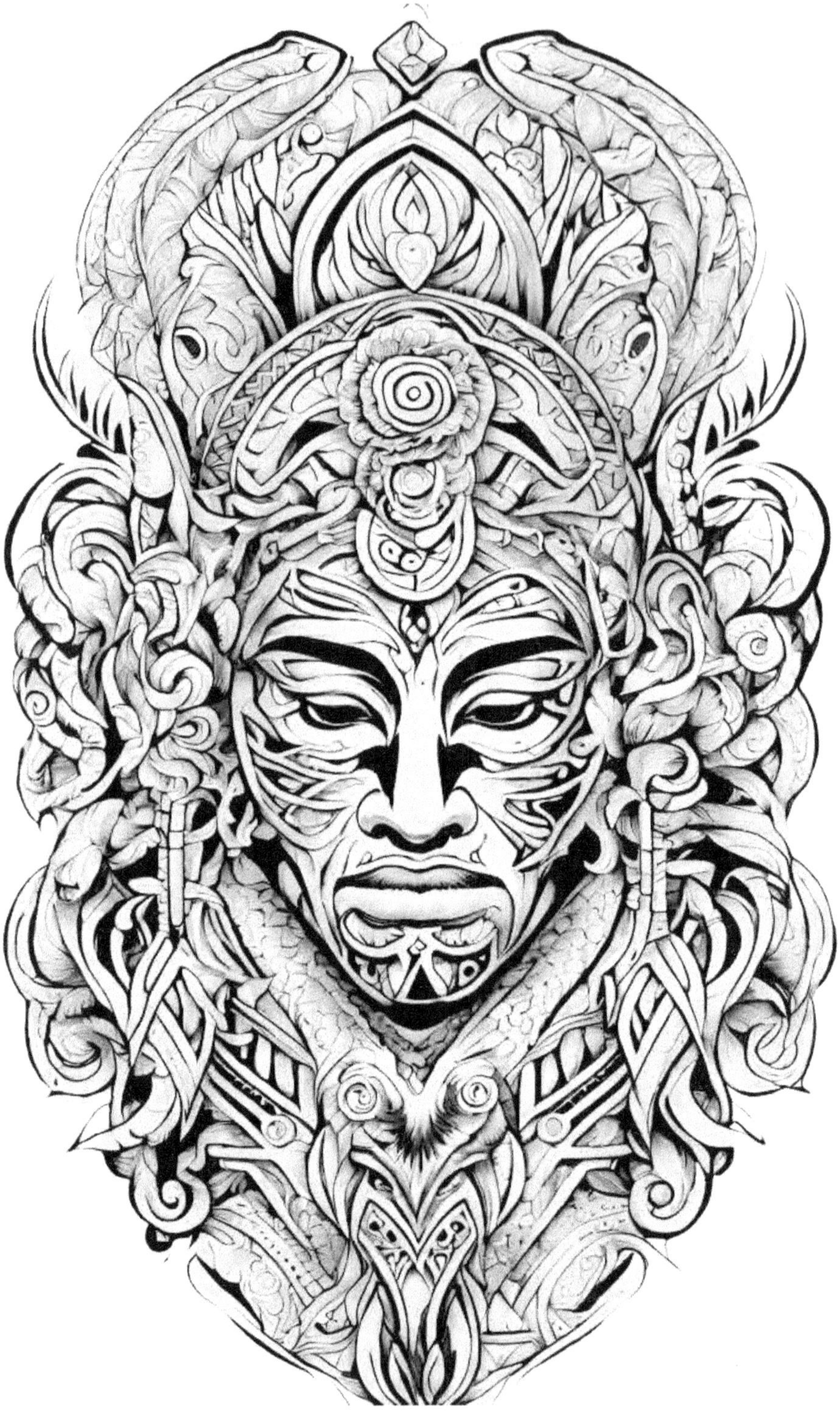

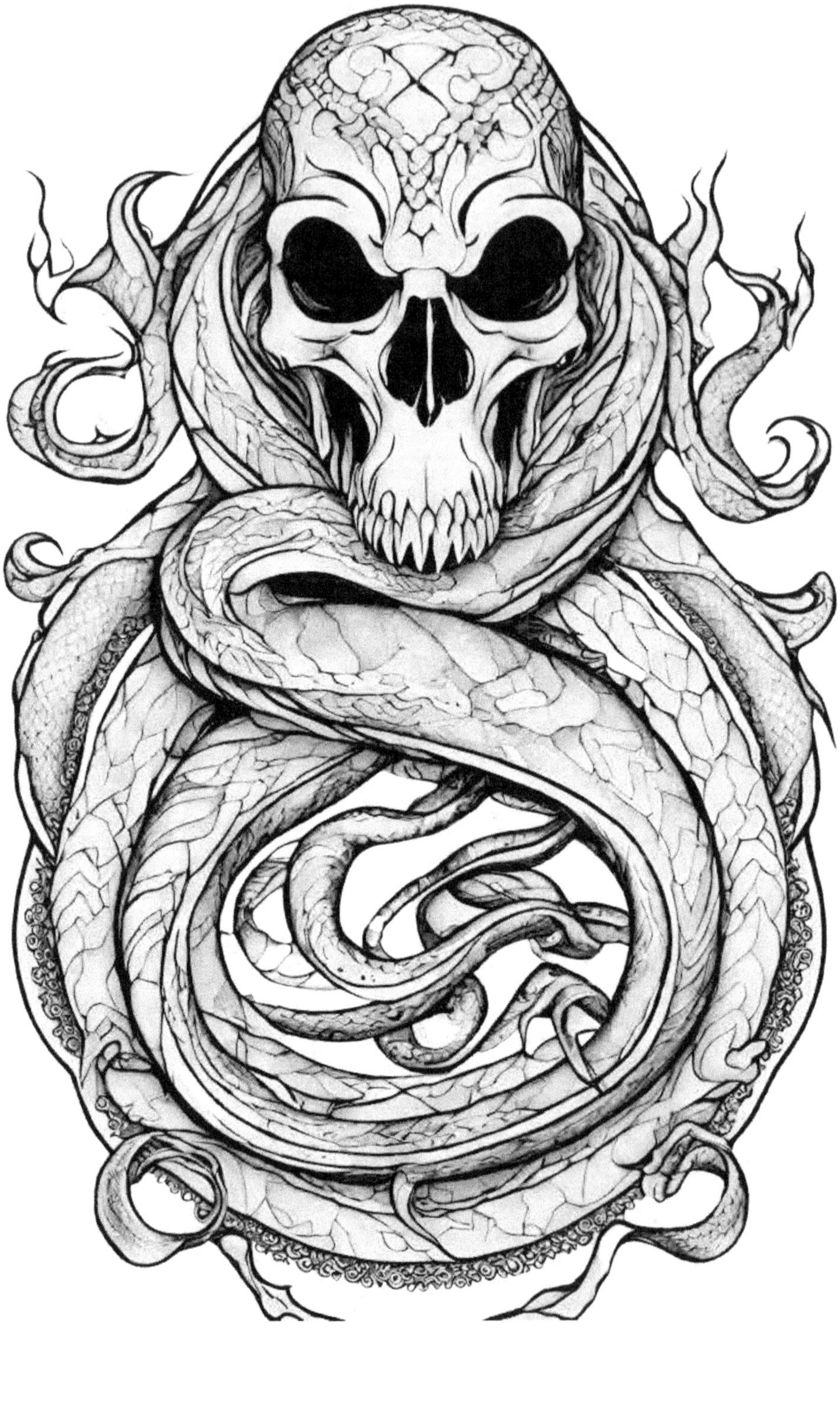

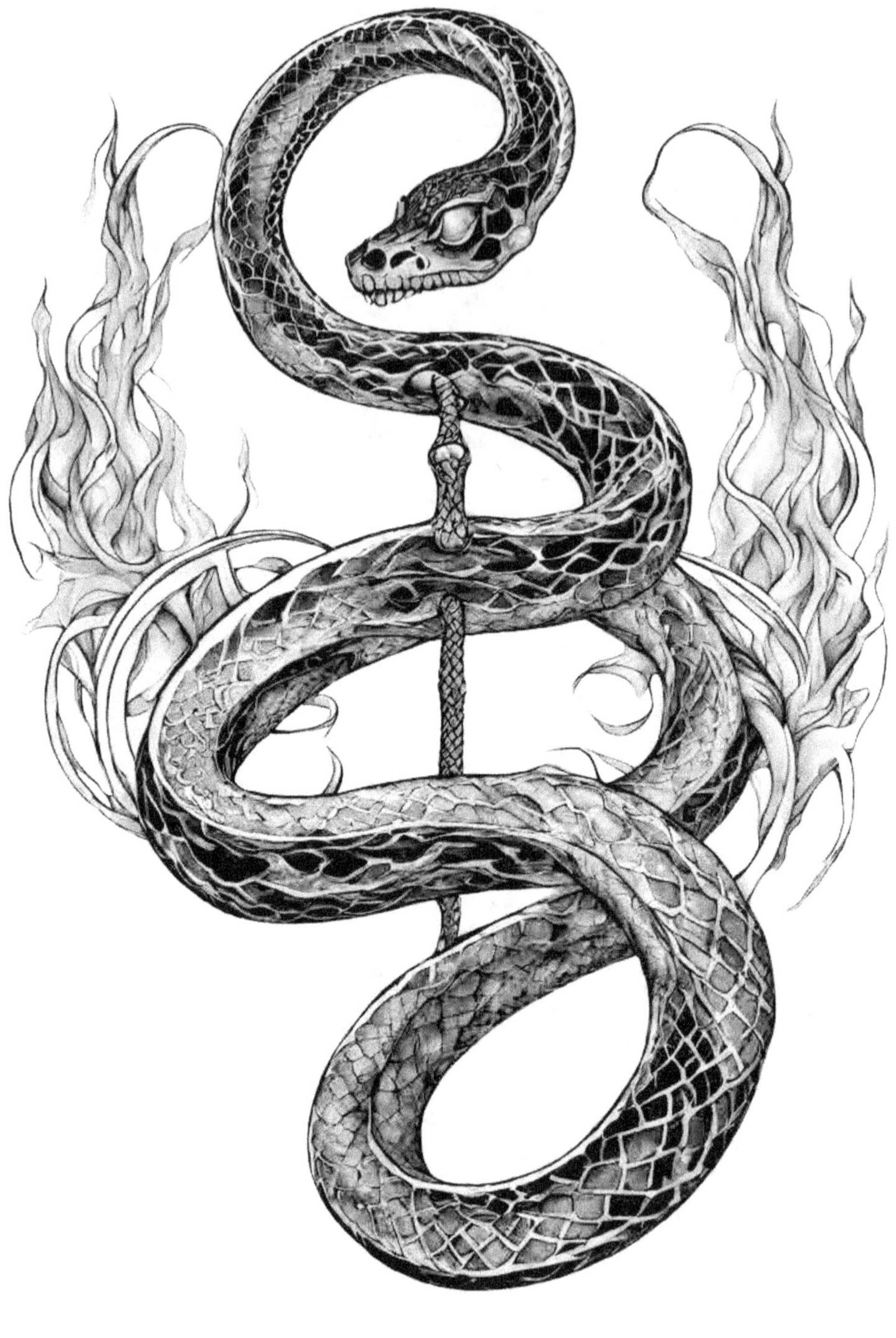

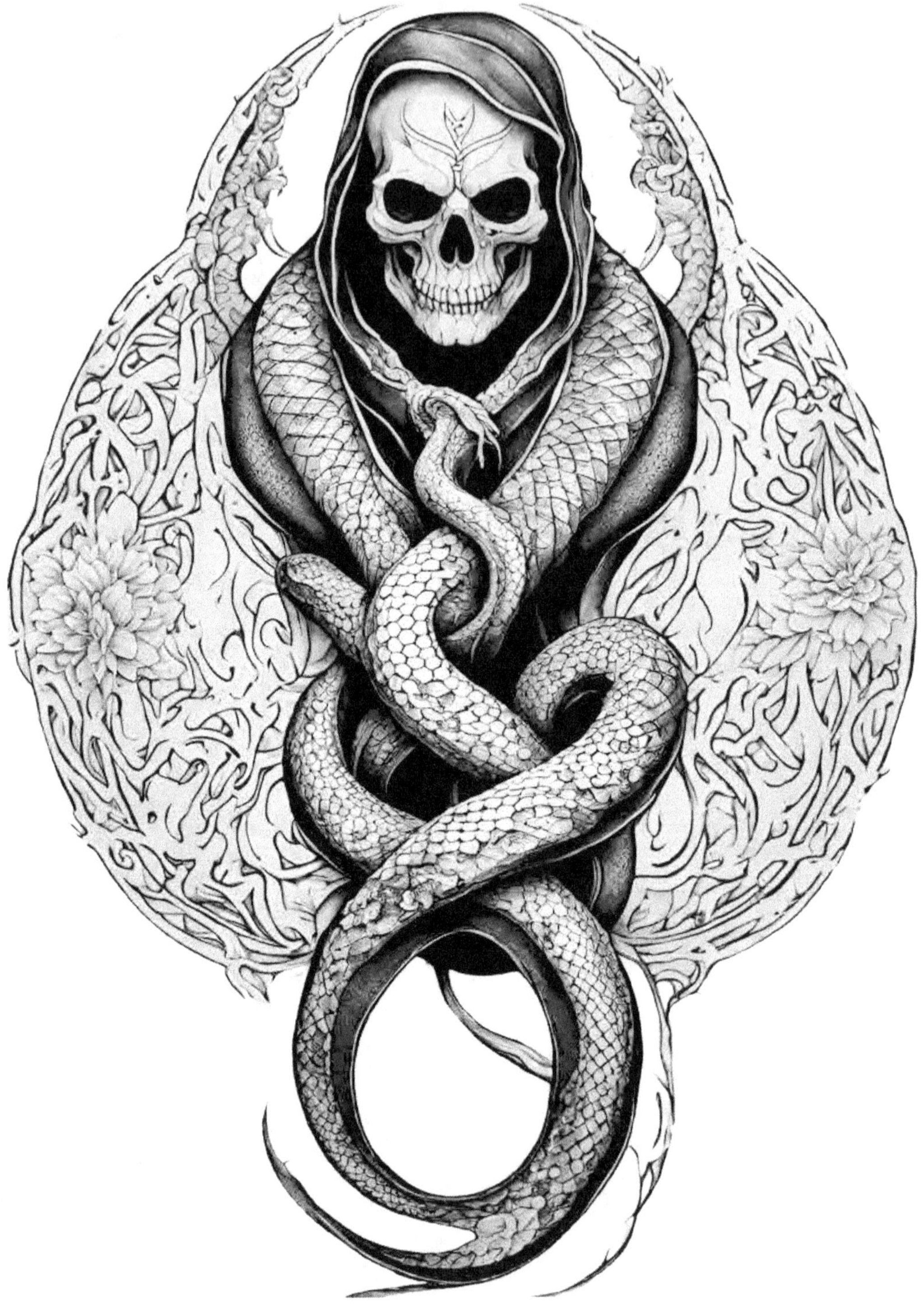

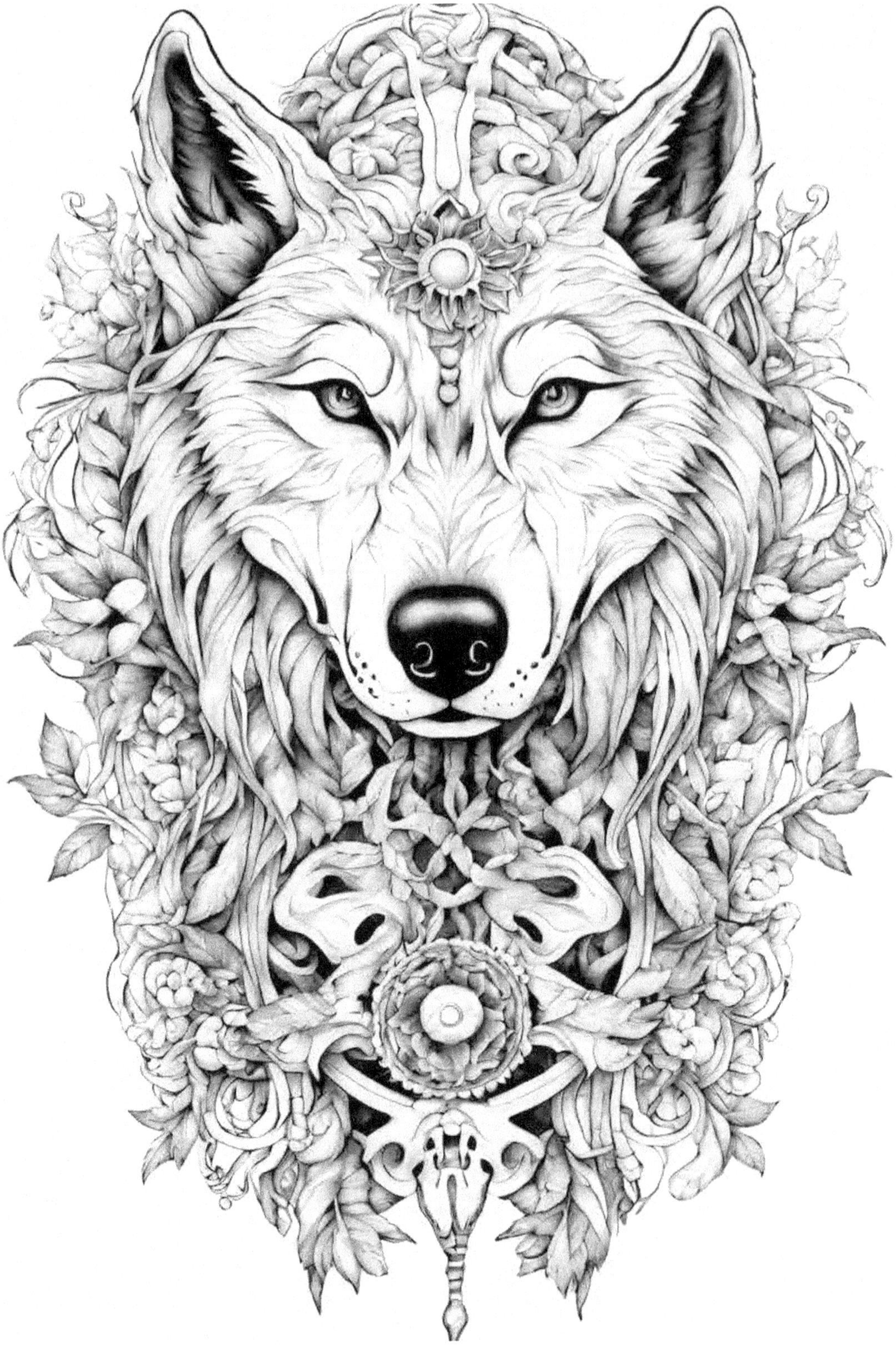

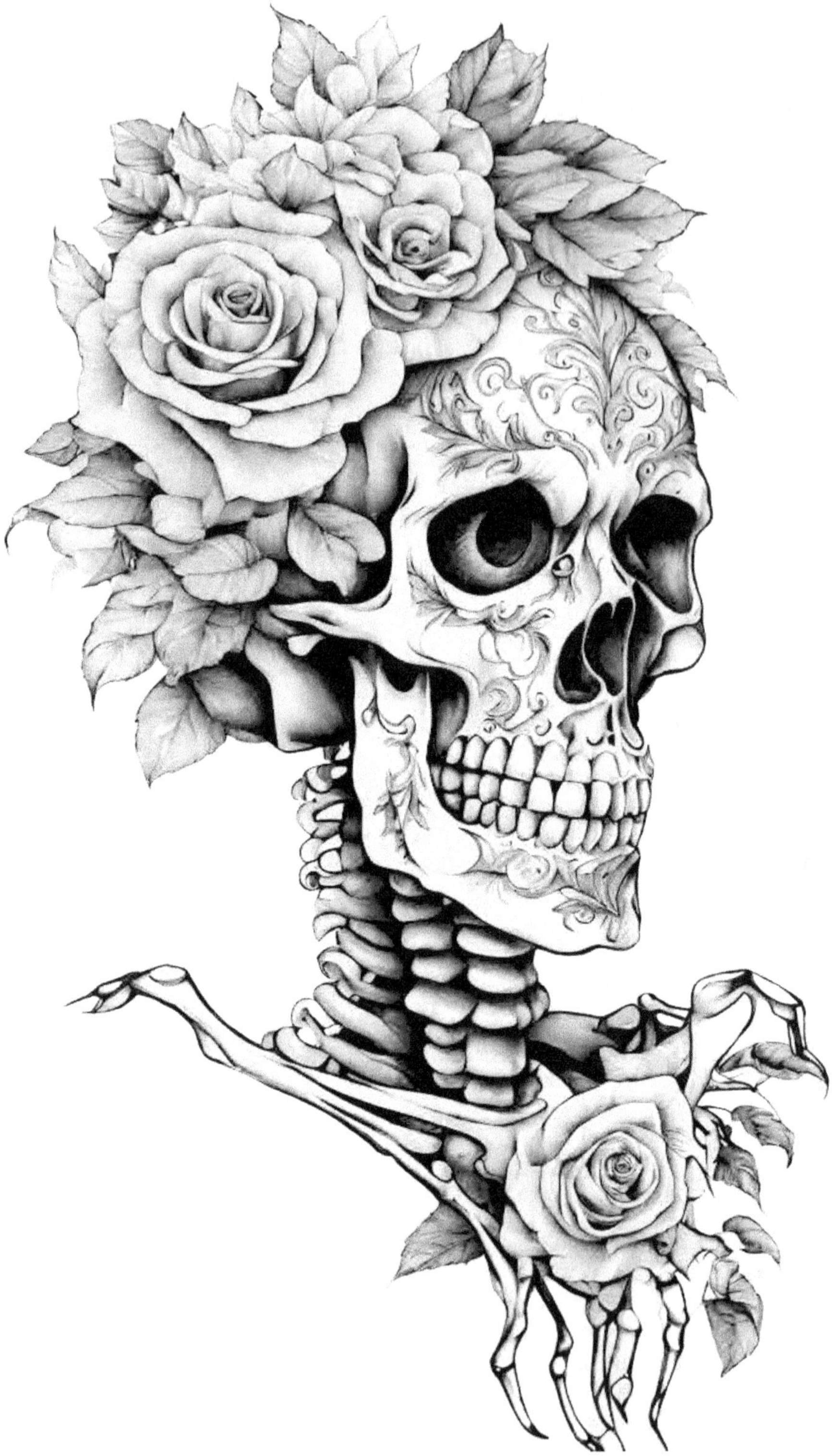

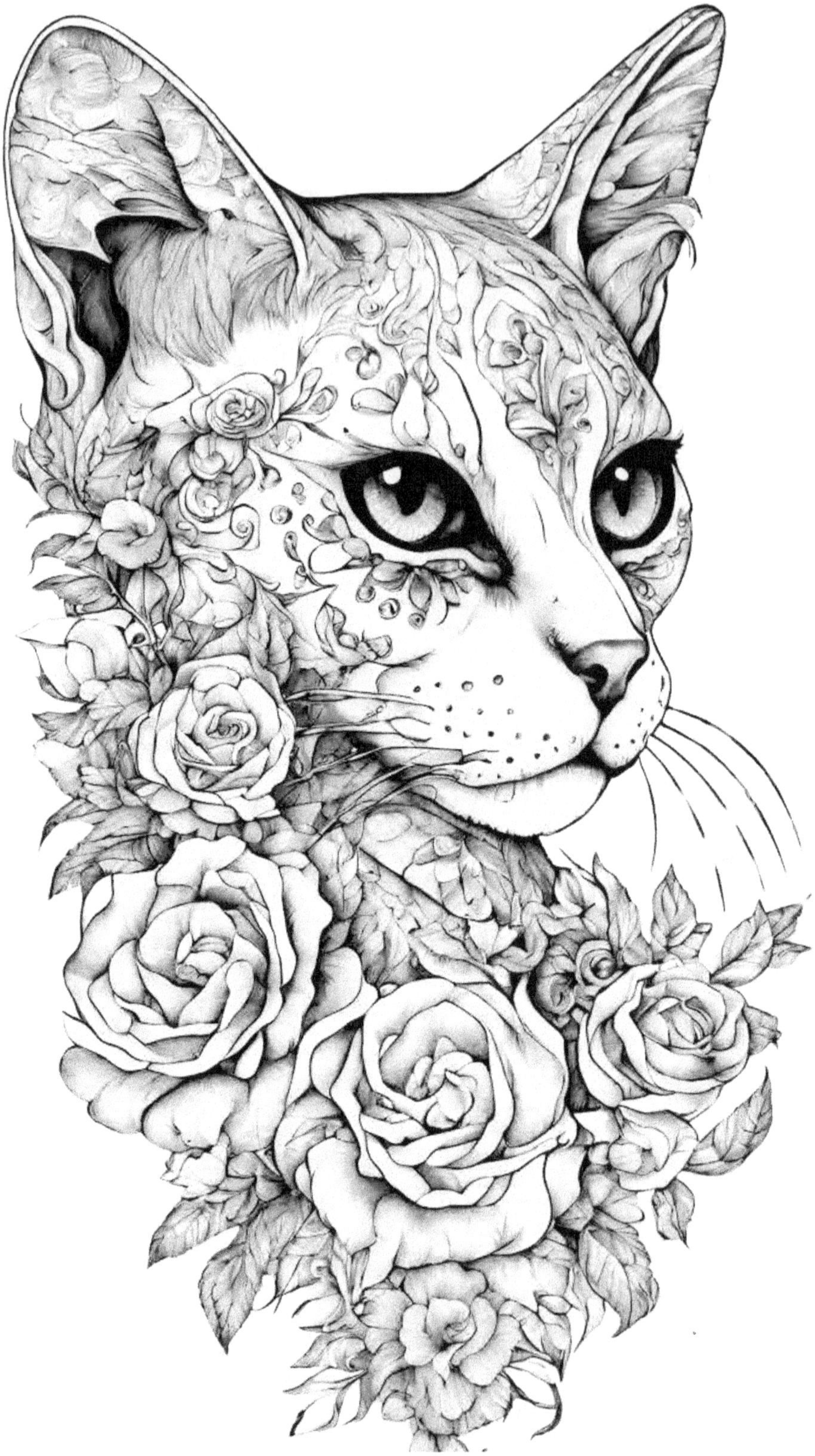

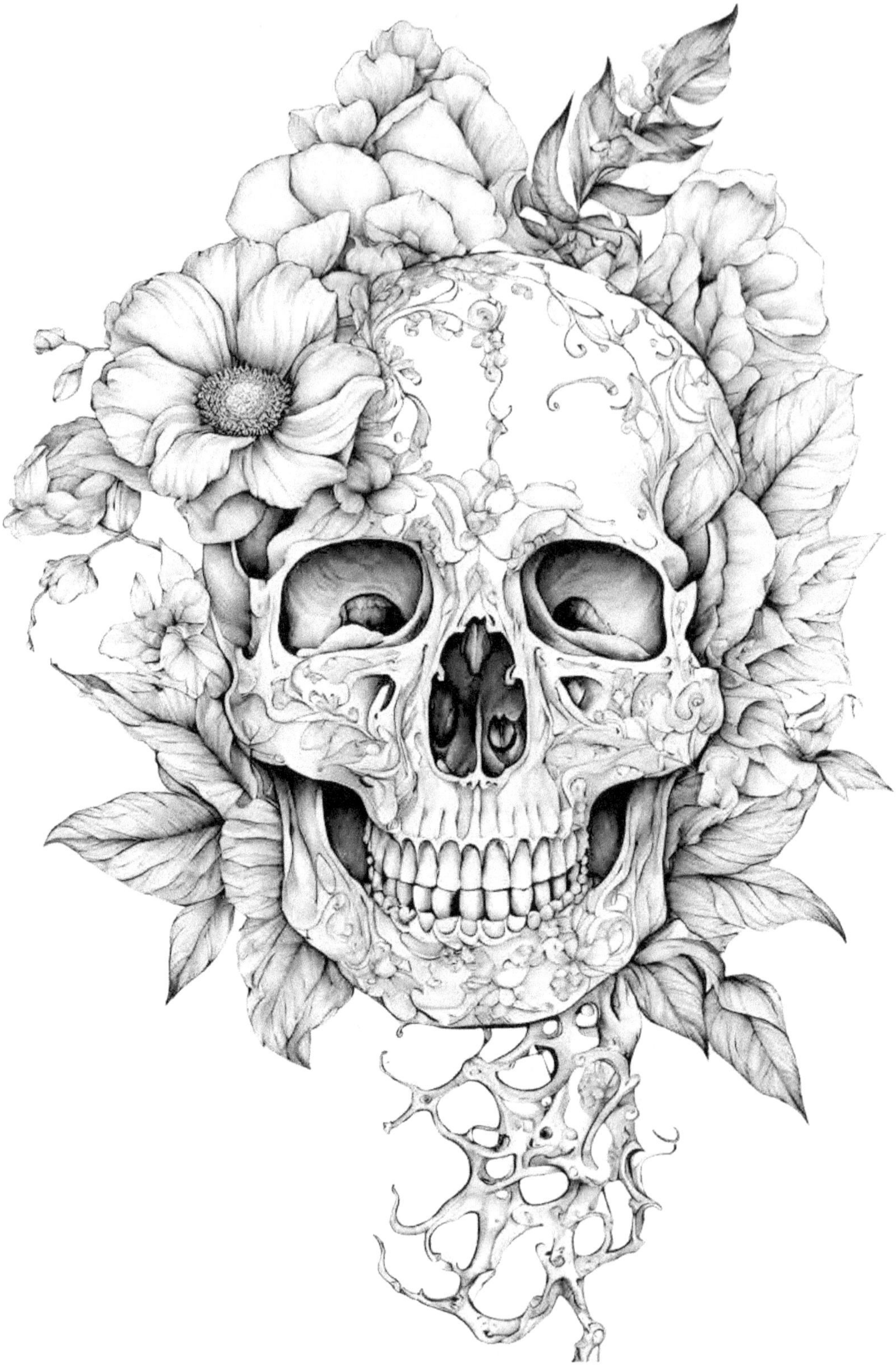

www.ingramcontent.com/pod-product-compliance
Lightning Source LLC
Chambersburg PA
CBHW081021240526
45471CB00018B/3923
* 9 7 9 8 3 2 3 7 8 4 4 1 7 *